PIEDRA is a song welling up from the earned wisdom of a life, a cry to the gods, a prayer to the ancestors and to the earth itself. Urrea's verses praise the living and the dead, knowing full well that " we toil/in the basement/of the angel factory." Just read "Breve Poema de Amor" and tell me you aren't in love. Just read PIEDRA and tell me the world you live in hasn't shifted on its axis.

—**Brian Turner**, author of *Here, Bullet*

That which cannot be destroyed — so it is, this is Urrea's Piedra Tao, Urrea's third eye swiveling across the cosmos & canyons, timeless in "this kernel of corn," an endless spiraling prayer of the rezanderas, an inky rosario of vision heat, caminatas, a sitting on the "oldest stone on the earth," as he writes he throws his arms up, cracks open his chest to the night stars and the sacred blaze of the "angel factory" — he chants, he whispers, tender and ragged on the "curve of cerulean blue" the poems, the book. The "Piedra," "arises "wild and free," this is ocean magic, re-stitched sizzling bullets of Zapata, you will eat seashell and taste "Belgian stamps," you will lean on wild wolves, smell their pelts, you will "feed iguanas," you will eat at the restaurant of Urrea's mysteries, unlock their ancient honeyed lips and smear your face upon them and their shadows will come to you and you will enter the life and lives of the blinking elements of Piedra consciousness forever. I absolutely love this book, these poems, these short-line and long-line, night and dawn painted teachings. An incredible pyramid and temple of word magic. Bravissimo! No doubt, no return.

—**Juan Felipe Herrera,**
Poet Laureate of the United States, Emeritus

PIEDRA

FLOWERSONG
PRESS

New Poems
by
LUIS ALBERTO URREA

FLOWERSONG
PRESS

FlowerSong Press

ISBN: 978-1-953447-19-7
Library of Congress Control Number: 2023930332

Published by FlowerSong Press
in the United States of America.
www.flowersongpress.com

Cover Photograph by Luis Alberto Urrea
Cover Design by Edward Vidaurre
Set in Adobe Garamond Pro

For Cinderella
y la familia.

For those who came before, and
for those who will come after.

Contents

Part I.

Part II.

Part III.

PART IV.

Ancestors, I fly for you.

—Rudolfo Anaya

Piedra

Part I.

Gloria Mundi

Mountains unseam,
split, spit red thunder, all life
in excess: the drop
of milk rises pearly
to nipple's peak
and trembles for
a mouth: living rain.

What need does
beauty have of us:
this kernel of corn
holds within itself
every milpa through time, cracked in mouse's teeth--
flea upon its back
wanders aspen glades of fur: obsidian ceremonial dagger
driven in through skin, sips
crimson platelets
from the same heart as mine.

Virgen de Guadalupe, pray for us.
Tonantzin, pray for us.
Malinche, pray for us.
Santa Sabina, pray for us.
Lola Beltran, pray for us.
Soldadera, pray for us.
Hechizera, pray for us.
Profesora, pray for us.
Despeinada, pray for us.
Chola, pray for us.
Pocha, pray for us.

Abuelita, pray for us.
Chingona, pray for us.
Llorona, pray for us.
Sor Juana, pray for us.
Bruja, pray for us.
Lesbiana, pray for us.
Detenida, pray for us.
Olvidada, pray for us.
Abandonada, pray for us.
Viuda, pray for us.
Hija, pray for us.
Hambrienta, pray for us.
Desaparecida, pray for us.
Asesinada, pray for us.
Guerrera, pray for us.
Madre, pray for us.

Poeta, pray for us
Now and in the hour of our death
In the glory of what you have given for us
In the promise of never forgetting
In the shelter of your shadow
Amen.

Letter to My Daughter Written When She was Three

Rosario,
this endless season
is so brief.

Once,
in Oklahoma midnight
on the road for days
half-way down the highway home,
I walked out to keep watch
on the Milky Way visible
for the first time since I'd cared to notice—
you have to be vigilant with God
at every turn, even if God
does not exist—that's your choice—
you can't let God get away with anything
because you are the silent partner
in this world-making—
so
at first that star-smear above
looked like electric smoke, or
some prairie fire back-lit
by the steer-horn moon, you know
it looked like a restless river of milk
spilled across dark meridians where you
flew down to us.

#

I was footloose on a gravel road
like a homesteader on stolen dirt, walking

the same direction as the sky river, just
not as far—though I bet the ants on that road thought it

about the size of heaven itself and I was some
thunder lizard: it was hay fields and frog ponds, the world:
deer stole sunflowers all night, barbed wire
drooped loose and sang in prairie winds like harps:
I wore sandals
that later I would wear
walking you down a desert gorge to a red river
and on the way back stood with your mother under
a hanging garden that wept
delicious water on our heads
in benediction.

Inside the Grand Canyon, once, I had decided—
should you ever come—to write this letter to you.
I sat on the oldest stone on earth, shared water and lunch
with Mexicans (you should know this: we find each other
no matter where we are), struggled back up
unable, I believed, to go on, until lightning
taught me different--daughter
when you can't anymore, you discover that you have
a mile uphill run still within you.

#

It's funny, the mysteries you will decipher
long after I am gone too far and too long
to hear what you have discovered, but know
that your presence
makes the world sacred—look, even
Oklahoma spiders in the holy cottonwoods
were the size of your pink hands
colored bright as bananas

and turquoise rings, and they played their webs
hung from low branches
like flamenco guitarists, right above the chokecherries,
arms thrown open to the winds: look, ducks
slumbering in invisible ponds were still

reflected in black shine: look, there was as much
gravel on this nameless road as there were stars
in that celestial patch where you descended to us:
how could I have known
that a light shaped like you
too small to be seen
saw us from above, clothed
in mysteries that would always be hidden,
had been blinked from God's dark eye
my child, my daughter, to lead
what will remain of us
when we have been summoned
away from you for a week or two
back home.

(Easter Sunday)

Zapata Haiku

Zapata met the Buddha
on the highway—
shot him.

Cielo

I loved you most
when you were empty

black obsidian
curve of cerulean thirst

open to drink
these earthly dreams

I loved you best
knotted into storms

wrathful green
about your business

of twisters floods
or after when your tears dropped

into the mouths of lilies:
you, have you come

for me now, is it time
so soon? you

who carried away Zapata
and my mother

who carried away the poets
of the Popol Vuh

have you opened
yourself

to carry me up
while I am still singing?

Continuum

With luck, somewhere
tonight I am already old

pensioned in a brown
room

a saggy bed and
300 notebooks

a shoebox of pictures
a jarrito of cool water.

On this same night, in San Diego
I am sixteen, naked

with the first notebook
on my bedroom floor

only Leonard Cohen
understanding anything of love

and I pause
writing about her

to smell her fresh
as dawn.

Just for one moment
we see each other

boy y viejo
through this page

and weep.

Marriage

For C

When I dream of you
I see us in a house
beside the sea

that we could never afford.
We sleep late,
a thing our kids and dogs

would never allow.
You wear that dress, that one from France
so full of gardens.

Mountains above you
are bright with aspens
and valleys of snow.

And you and I have remained
young, a place we are being
cast out from with no return.

But we laugh at that,
we will one day awaken
without a clock,

awaken from this lovely skin
arise like morning
into mornings more wild and free.

E.Z.

Alerta.
Este es el corrido de Emiliano Zapata.
He dreamed of revolution on the main drag
selling Chiclets from cardboard trays
to turistas in fat Chevy SUVs—
afterward, when he counted up his centavitos
to buy paper kites & a wooden top,
instead
he bought
a .44 bullet.

LA CERTEZA DE CANELA

Tienes la certeza de canela—
En ti las macetas pintadas
Del sur arden
Con el fuego brotado de geranios.

Confieso que la memoria
De tu boca de cerezas
Es una fogata
Que tumba la noche en cenizas.

Tu voz, bocanada de humo,
Hilo de música y suspiro,
El relámpago de tu sabor
Cortan huellas en mi piel.

Tu te, tu lluvia,
Me dejaron boqueando
En la orilla de este mar,
Esta costa perfumada.

Llueve, llueve,
Llevame
Permiteme nadar.

Natural Selection, National Avenue

And white dudes said black dudes smelled funky and black dudes said Mexican dudes had stupid accents and smoked horse shit cigarettes and all other dudes including white dudes and pinoy dudes and portagee tuna boat dudes sons of fishermen threw punches if you went to the wrong corner especially if you were some leftover pachuco in your ridiculous clothes and catholic dudes fought pencil necked hallelujahs on the corner and some dudes pulled knives because thank god nobody much had guns yet but when they did logan heights shot barrio logan who shot hoyo maravilla who shot del sol who shot highriders who chased lowriders and del sol set fire to my nephew under the 805 off-ramps and my dearest friend had to hide in balboa park toilets to make love with boys to be safe and I remember finding old books in my apartment that I tried to read in the laundry room across the big concrete slab where no dudes came around except Jerome that one dude who stomped my kitten but everywhere you looked red ants and black ants met on the slab one side from the south and one side from the north and perpetual war busied the middle every day without fail and after hours of fighting red heads and black heads and legs and feelers lay scattered yet somehow still talking shit just like us and no wonder I prayed every day that St. Jude and Jesus and Teresa of Cabora would lead me into something new—
My first poems.

El Gran Silencio

Vivimos desamparados
En este mundo flotante—
El desierto es puro vidrio

Y todos los caballos
Cabalgan y sangran—
Insistente quebradura de cristal.

Bajo la tierra,
Todos los muertos
Estan alegres—

Pos mira, Compa,
Esas sonrisas
Que traen.

La musica mas dulce
Es el silencio.

This Deserted Hour

Volo ut sis.
—Agustine

Hush now.
Quiet now.
Nemontemi.
These are the days
        of silence, this
        the deserted hour
        between years.
Hush.

All songs are whispered,
even the raven's.
Seasons balance
        over this chasm
        in time.
Hunters flee
Xochitonal, Flowered Monster
of the underworld—Uayab, devil of these
lost hours: Quinames, known in Israel, giants of renown,
        awaken in the Nephilim earth.

Watchers await.

Be still.
Tally
 the count of
your days: today, your hours
complete this cycle
of your infinite dance.

We cannot be known. Yet we sing.
We live in deserted lands.
We see our reflections
in black iron walls
that keep us from the shadows
or our mothers.
We have two souls
 we try to stitch together again
with shadows.

Anything

anything in this hush
            anything at all
could happen. This big hush.

Be still.

The Shortest Prayer-Song

The shortest prayer
Song the Mexica sang
Went this way:

Nie.

"Nee-Yeh."

It rolls forever
Over us still, fills
Ruined choirs, jungled
Temples.

It breaks the dark
And fills all silence,
Our daily cry:

I Am.

Part II.

Babylonian Alphabets: A Poet's Notebooks

It's how high you are and the time it takes to heal.
—Catherine Wheel

Fill your paper with the breathings of your heart.
—Wordsworth

A white iris
Painted by
Hawk dung.

—Buson

This is how words work around here:
nothing but hope. Even
In despair. Just words
in search of vision.

#

Annotated notes
on the education of
a foolish soul:
we too
can imitate plovers
even on the old man's
beach.

#

it is a long walk
across silent plains
carrying
this box of song

#

we toil
in the basement
of the angel factory

#

My elders left me
land-mines of guilt
as if they knew
these would blow my feet off
to teach me a lesson.

#

every second
is Now
for the hummingbird

#

Issa said the world drowns in haiku.
He also said Simply Trust.
Lots of homework, amigo.

#

lizard
spares

chirping
cricket

tilts
head
and
listens

#

Western Lunch Chinese Café.

A Xicana with one cool braid in her raven hair tells a man at the next table about her mom's new boyfriend. As usual, I am addicted to the music of the stories. Everything smells of mu-shu.

She asks the cooks at the counter to make her a chocolate milk-shake. When it comes, she stirs sugar into it. A beat woman sitting near her is saying, "I wouldn't be his whore-bait so he got pissed off." Suddenly, the man sitting with the chocolate Xicana tells her, "I'm a crazy idiot."

They get up to leave, and he says, "I feel like a zombie, Baby-Doll."

My fortune cookie says: YOU WILL SOON BE RICHER DAY BY DAY.

But I am already rich.

#

Mind
Distracted
By heart.

#

One must love Carl Phillips. He writes: "Story, versus information. Lyric, versus didactic. Long, periodic sentences, verses clipped, straightforward ones. Catalpa trees aren't hawthorns. I'm not the man I was." (In THEN THE WAR.)

I remember a moment at Breadloaf, which felt like an unlikely home for me over the years, and a place Carl seemed to own, elegantly. I was in the barn, where I did my conferences. Always a fire going, always coffee, often various bakery goods. In one corner, a rattan throne that was so 1967, so pretentious, I had to sit there for my meetings. And I was sitting near a small group of workshoppers gathered at a little table to my right. They were talking about Carl. We writers are a terrible bunch of snoops—Kim Stafford calls what we do "eloquent listening." They were fretting about the poet's level of affection for them.

Suddenly, he appeared, striding resolutely toward the coffee machine.

One young woman leapt up and said, "Mr. Phillips?"

He paused, tipped his head.

"We were worrying," she said, "that you mean much more to us than we do to you."

He didn't even blink.

"Yes," he said and got his coffee and walked back out.

Clipped, straightforward sentences indeed.

#

my garden's
loveliest blossom's
a weed

#

Fogbank recedes
a pine tree steps forward
and another.

#

After 1,000,000 American plague dead and counting, I resolve
to see anew, to take sight into my hand,
to spill the blood of the sacred wound of witness
onto the snowbanks of these notebooks, these
watchtowers, these whispers to the distracted
angels, this record of careless rambles and hard dark
and drives into the vanishing point.
V-8 Interceptor full of ink.

#

Dude—Rilke said, "I live my life in widening circles that reach out around the world." But the first circle is right here, right now. And we learn how to live within its expanding border.

#

I will wrap lines
around you, cover
your tongue in song

#

Atchafalaya Headlines.

Beau Jocque on the radio / "make it stink" / creatures crunch / roil & churn / flitter-flick, fly, wings slither-tongues, swamp-scaled / cool blue swimmers in hot water / crawlers collate, file fever forms in the funky cabinet / "can you really make it stink?" / chumbling chooglin' midnight fangs poison frogs all afumble / wet / undertow poet reptiles rattle tails cottonmouth boogaloo / anarchist crawlies got that cricket thang cookin' / "Is it stinkin'?" / verb, noun, drowned adjective, dragonfly adverb zydeco grammar / wetland of the heart.

#

I ran to places I had not
Seen before and there
Found my characters
Awaiting me, already
Written.

#

Overheard, Santa Fe:

NASCAR mechanic stands and says

They's just two things you need to know
about God.

One:
they is one.

Two:
you
ain't
it.

#

water too
started like us—
clear, free of sin

#

Chi.

It is that time of year when the ponds freeze over. The ice is greasy-looking down beside the foundry beside the expressway. Gray as fog. Little streams along the road are white now, and stilled. Grass breaks underfoot. Is there a message? Does this earth speak to us? Bare trees stand against the walls of glass and steel, scriptures written in Babylonian alphabets.

#

I have collected words like a boy with a box of seashells. They sit bright in my hands. They taste of salt. I don't know yet what to do with them, how to put them together. But I will. I can hear them start to rhyme 20, 30 years down the road. Here are some of them: interstate, mariposa, saguaro, night-hawk, Oglala, kotodama, kintsugi, sabi, ilhuicac tlaxcaltzintli, pumpjacks.

#

I am cutting paragraphs
out of my life & mounting them
here like 1938
Belgian stamps.

#

Dude—Rudy Anaya said: "You are innocent until you understand."

#

Waiter overheard at a salad bar: "I gotta get a better fix on my angle."

#

Writers
Are
Magpies.

And everything is shiny.

#

I write to meet
the wild wolf and not
flee its hot breath

#

Sometimes, writing makes you feel like a snail with no shell on patrol in a world made of salt.

#

Cooking is song.
Eating is song.
You never stop singing.

#

Petaluma, CA. As we stood in the Whole Foods parking lot, a white van sped into the drive and skidded to a halt in front of us. The driver's window came down. There is that second when you think there is a drive-by shooting about to happen. Inside, however, everyone was dressed up like The Incredibles. Complete with over the head face masks. The driver was Mr. Incredible. He hung his big rubber face out and bellowed, "Everyone all right here?" We gave him the thumbs-up. "Is everybody safe?" We nodded. He slammed it into gear and sped back out of the lot.

#

2 dragonflies
part before the windshield
opening the portal

#

Rubble
this notebook
is rip-rap.

#

Dude—Myriam Gurba said: "During every spiritual journey, there's bound to be a little bit of foolishness."

#

What is that feeling after the first cup of coffee after a troubling dream after a hard night? A night that echoes as it recedes. Writer, get to work.

#

How do you love this world? How do you, after you've ingested all its cruel lessons, all the poison and disappointment and rage and betrayal of it? Is it accomplished through religion? Do you pray without ceasing? The oak tree is always praying. But how do you love this life? How do you honor this life? I have chosen something very small. Writing. Watch it grow.

#

I would
Cut myself open
And pour you into the wound.

#

Dream 12/8/81

It was a shoreline of multicolored stones, white terraces and tide pools. I saw a blind man who put down his white cane and leaned over the sea wall to touch the faces of jeweled iguanas.

“But they’ll bite you,” I said.

“I must feed them,” he replied.

And he did.

#

abandoned trailer
sardine can beside the highway
ghosts packed in oil

#

Poetry’s market is the heart—
It’s small, but it is always open.

#

Rain
        Rain
                Rain
                        Rain….

Columbines!

#

When the poem wants to hatch, a poet will come into the nest.

#

Someone wrote in this old Edna St. Vincent Millay book: "Too much weeping! Tears, tears, idle tears!" But my favorite marginalia is someone with a purple pen who wrote in sad crooked letters beneath a Sharon Olds poem about sex: "I was happy once." I foolishly believe they are my friends.

#

There's a dome of pages circling above us,
gulls of the ink ocean, and they stay just out of reach.
A million pale wings, fluttering. Hurry—
put out some bread.

#

Life grows into our words from the bottom. You put them in soil. You're rich and dark and smell like summer. You're vital. Feel those roots go in. Now grow a masterpiece.

#

Faculty meeting
I am forced
To daydream of magpies.

#

Dude—Jim Harrison said: "To write a poem you must first create a pen that will write what you want to say. For better or worse, this is the work of a lifetime."

#

God, I need you wild—
I cannot have you golfing,
I cannot buy you white loafers.

#

God, my students asked
why writers see you in trees
when they can't.

#

God, whose language
do you accept in prayer—
crow, mountain, mine?

#

God, the hostages heard
about your mercy
before they were killed.

#

God,
I am here.
Use me.

#

Geese cry at midnight--
Far from me
My wife sleeps alone.

#

I am listening.

#

First, accept silence.

#

Vision beats theory.

#

Say it anyway.

#

I'm headed yonder.

#

Dude--Rilke said: "And God said to me, write."

#

Wandering is the path to words. Drove to Quartzite AZ, then up Cottonwood Creek Road all the way to Joshua Tree. All attendant scenic wonders were present. Rocks formed Nephilim skulls that peered over the hills. Two mile long freight trains going each way paused to stare at each other. Joshuas raised their spiky hands like fans at a U2 concert. Dear trucks settled into blood-tinged quartz rubble, punched through by scores of bullets, interiors pebbled with decades of fossilized kangaroo-rat turds. Ripped seats still coughing out wasps. I hiked along the path of the manifest perfection of cacti. Pen flying. I sped to Blythe—was amazed to find Black music fans inside Utopia Records buying Funkadelic LPs, flipping through the Rap bins. Not a single straw cowboy hat in sight. Last best vision: over the roof of a motorhome on the same highway home as me, the vast grinning face of a T.rex. I chased the sunset, escaping to the western sea where I came from.

#

Words, of course, are each one a small song.

#

What is he thinking—
that old man in the snow
staring south.

#

Underwear
on her hip—
Modigliani.

#

The most dangerous
Leap of faith—
"I love you."

#

writers in rain
huddle under stories
and dream of home

#

My right-wing MAGA friends think I have a lib agenda. When I write about respect for the wanderer, about clothing the widow, about feeding the hungry and giving kindness to migrant children, they send me correctives, threats and insults. But this isn't political. This is my religion.

#

I shouted, "Deer!" It was a bus stop bench. Undaunted, I sped toward the eastern Colorado high plains.

Just after tornadoes. And The Angel of Writing revealed herself to me. Her sword was sharper than the wind. She gave me a dispensation. You can't touch me now.

#

There is a spirit of writing. Did you know? A real spirit. And it's interactive. You make a mistake thinking writing is some kind of sport, some warfare. If there is a spirit of writing, you keep it alive. You are its life support system. You give breath and life to it. Nobody said it would be easy. Imagine how hard aspens have to work to suck water out of bedrock to make those golden coins shiver in the sun.

#

Dead gas station.
Dead motor court.
Dead truck.
Dead bones.
All of them white.
All of them shouting poems.

#

Someone once told me: it is good
to know the terrain so you understand
how lightly you should tread.

#

The poet's mouth in rain—
rising steam and
the word "cutbank."

#

blank page—
field of snow
awaiting ravens

#

suffered early—
chose joy
for the finish

#

Dude—Zadie Smith said: "The very reason I write is so that I might not sleepwalk through my entire life."

#

Writing:
sometimes you're a falcon
on a western breeze
closing on a pheasant at
200 mph: sometimes
It's the Atchafalaya
and you're wearing lead shoes
and here come the gators.

#

being angry
is so much
easier

#

I called Basho.
He confirmed.
He was the one who said,
"The journey itself is home."
I told him the critics in my department
Think words like "journey" are empty cliches.
"Ask me," Basho said,
"If I care."

#

Every new year
Repeats unchanging—
The week my father died.

#

Surrender to ceremony.

#

Nothing is lost.

#

Joy takes discipline.

#

Prevailing's what prevails.

#

Strangers hug me.

#

Wabi sabi everything.

#

This is all I know of grace. Chekhov once said something like: to a chemist, dung is as important to a landscape as roses. I think of where we have come, after all our torments and trials, after our despair and hope, after waiting for the call from the oncologist, after all the birthdays, after all the impossible bills and rejections and embarrassments. We are in a great bald field. And we are essentially alone, or believe we are. We are lonesome. And a cow or an elk or a javelina pauses and deposits a ration of feces on the ground. Flies come right away—we are disgusted by them, yet their eyes are each 1,000 prisms that reflect 10,000 colorful mountains. And metal green beetles come to lay eggs. And a westerly wind spins up and brings three dandelion seeds and daisy seeds and mushroom spores all the way from your childhood and they catch on the edge of the crap and settle in. It rains. They sprout. Unexpectedly, a raven flies overhead and launches a dropping that contains one cherry pit. That pit falls into your small accidental garden. More rain. Moonlight and sunlight and heat and snow and more rain and the cherry pit sprouts. And the weeds around your cherry tree bloom and their blossoms bring bees and butterflies and migrating hummingbirds. Before you know it, you have an oasis that becomes a meadow. That becomes a cherry orchard. That creates a small wood when bison bring cottonwood fluff in their fur. They dig wallows that fill with ground water and become small lakes. You are the settler who comes into the virgin forest and drinks that sweet water and make a home and open your notebook. This is how it works. That's the best I can do. That's all I know about grace.

#

Fill your pen with love or don't bother picking it up.

#

Dude—Le Guin said: "To witness fully, and be thus the altar of the thing witnessed."

Part III.

Arbor

1. Every bush is burning.

2. Each flaming tree
beneath the mirror
of the earth
is a naked reflection
of itself, standing
into the air
                of the ground.

3. All trees
are both trees and
empty spaces
in the air
shaped exactly
like trees.

4. Child
            we too
are empty spaces
in the sky
waiting
            to be filled.

5. She's pregnant!
Our deep pleasure
drew a soul's flight
from beyond the sun.

In the earth of my
bride, a
pomegranate
clear
    crimson
        ripens.

Daughter, come—
we found a name for you
and we call you
        through dark
        golden arc
        around Mars

      you taste the moon
      already seeking
      milk

fall like a maple seed
spin
into your mother.

6. Wife:
    Earth:
      Sea:
        Forest:
          Horizon:
            Home:
              Madre.

7. The clock awaits you. The trees.

Baseball. Chocolate.
David Bowie and sleeping late.

Broken toes await you. And dogs.

Books
perch like doves and ravens.
Waves.
                    Sunflowers.
Fire.

And we
who have opened the soil.
Who have a little water for you
and so many stories.
Everything waits.

So come.

Breve Poema de Amor

That day I only desired
To lay my tongue across your back,
To lift your summer dress
And smell the gardens
Along your legs.

I knew between your breasts
You hid a secret heat
That would make the world abate
If I could only earn
The honor of it spread across my lips.

Late, when I came to you wanting water,
You dipped a drop from your deep shadow
And drew your essence
Across my name.

Congregation

We face light alone.
No crowds at Revelation.
Only the loneliest
Clouds of solitude—
Which is our reward.
Every congregation is made
Of one. Alone,
And thus connected.
Done in by truth
That leaves no place to hide
Until its will be done.

Deserta

If you should see
a Sonoran river
dance across
the Pinacate
desert

it is only the shadow
of a wandering
woman

bend your mouth
to that water—
there is enough in her
to save you both
if you'd
only let her

in her
you find smooth stones
gold
her rapids
are alive with
dragonflies

listen to her

when she sighs

she is singing the oldest
lullaby

give her shade
give her shelter
give her your hand
protect her from the engines

risk your blood
for her—
she is your sister

no matter what
she asks of you
say yes.

El Gran Silencio

Carnales,

Vivimos Desamparados
En este mundo flotante—
En este desierto de vidrio

Donde los caballos sangran
Y cada paso es acompañado
Por la insistente

Quebradura de cristales.
Bajo la tierra sagrada,
Todos los muertos están felices—

Pos mira como esos cabrones
No dejan de sonreír.
Aqui la musica

Es silencio.

Mexikarmik Bardo

The prayer wheel turned,
        The medicine wheel downtown
Scattered when the invaders came

        Down Broadway in their trokas—
We did not yet have the wheel
        Except for prayers. Still

We dropped those wagons
        And rode slow, our lifters
Making Impalas rear up like war horses

        Candy-apple flaked
Cruising las ruinas
        Low and slow, spraying runes

On stupid walls. Oye, carnal—
        Ya sabes the soul in its flight
Passes into

        And out of this karmic
Border. All souls who behold us
        Yearn to be us

But to be Raza
        Survival satori
Is the only way to enter.

Om namah shivaya.
Rifamos con safos.

Xochicuicatl.
Shakti.
Ora pro nobis.
Amen.

Mijita en Nueva York

Her first visit—she is six.
On a tour bus because she gets tired,
Showing her the great Manhattan Island.

On the Loisaida
A rat struggles
Through a saggy fence with a shred
Of pizza dangling from its mouth
And scrambles through weeds
And broken bottles

And my daughter cries

"Look! A happy bunny
Is hopping through the flowers!"

State Prison Lamentation

Inmate workshop, New Mexico Desert. Doing that thing—
That writer/convicts thing with words & the guards
Lighten up & bring in pizza—poetry & stories & soda
For the hard-case homies white & brown & one Warlock
w/ sharpened teeth & a split tongue who says to us,
"Guess what I can do with this."

Those locked-down pintos everybody's scared of
Saved their extra chicken wings & sugar & pepper packets
For their bros still in cages who couldn't get any fancy
Visiting writer treats. That was a workshop too, of
Course—bright samples for mouths who longed for flavor.
And when the guards collected our trash to carry outside
The walls to the dumpsters, a wise-ass grabbed 2 bags
& jumped in line with them & said, "I got this, Cap!
Let's go! You dudes just open the gates & I'll carry this
Shit right out for ya!" Everybody laughed. The main guard
Said, "You clown" to him. "Prison humor," shaking his head.

After an hour it was time for a cigarette break. The guard were
Gone from the room & the door to the Yard opened electronically
& I headed out with the inmates who were looking to smoke a few &
I wandered around the Yard & the weight benches & followed
My favorite bank robber to the chain link fence where the homies
Could stare at the desert, wild & free, nothin' out there but
100 miles of liberty & he said, "See that little ol' hill right there?"
Yeah. "Ain't but a mile away." Yeah, I see. "Well, my Mama's
Got a little rancho right behind that hill." Wow. "I stand here
Every day and wish I was there. It's just a mile away. If I could bust
Through this fence I could walk home right now & eat supper with
Her." Damn, bro!

He took a puff. Leaned over. "I ain't gonna lie," he said. "I robbed
That fuckin' bank! But I miss my Mama." We started to laugh
When the door banged back open like some war drum
& four guards ran to us & grabbed me and yelled, "Are you insane!"
They hooked my arms & levitated me backwards. "Visitors don't go on
The Yard! You wanna be killed?" I was flying backward.
The bank robber flicked away his cig and called, "See ya later--
Under that hill."

They all stared
& I vanished
& the door slammed
& all was silence.

The Gospel of the Birds

But ask the animals, and they will teach you,
or the birds in the sky, and they will tell you.

—Job 12: 7

Suddenly awake before the blind red eye of dawn has opened, wet across your throat, your chest, the hollows of your collarbone small pools of what might be water, and your thought again is sutures, and you rise so as not to disturb the one who loves you or all the others in your house who fear the word that rhymes with "dancer" and who, in their own ways have borne this siege beside you. So you creep into the bathroom, alien now in its dull comforts and hated mirrors from which an old man you do not know stares back wearily and you see blood and your body's wine spilling

from a fresh mouth in your throat and you don't know what is happening now—so much has already happened and your hand shakes and you are ashamed of this child-like terror and the beloved dead you call out to for help might be with you and might not and you fashion a nest for this cascade from toilet paper and you gather your clothes in the dark and creep downstairs to wake no-one, hand to your traitor throat like some heroine in a silent movie—but then, violence: a bird crashes into your big window hard as a thrown rock while the sky pearls. You can just see it fallen on the bricks.

You open the door and step out—the bricks are cold—and he lies at your feet, on his side, white chest and piebald flanks, one wing splayed like a discarded paper kite. You bend to him and he suddenly resurrects, his head bending back to you, mouth open, eyes blind as dawn. You let go of your throat and cup him, hot, in your tainted hands, he doesn't fight, but you want him to live more than anything in the world, you want him warm and strong and his ragged claw finds you in the nest of your hands and clutches your wedding ring finger and you pull him to your chest and whisper hope to him and he relaxes and suddenly, his two-stroke heart astounds you with its powerful beat: alive, alive, alive, alive. Ferocious, there: alive, alive, alive, alive. Your shirt collar is wet. The sky above is brightening. Birds have come to the garden as if seeking him but you know that's just a prayer, and when you open your hands, he is whole, he leaps into the light, he lands in your maple tree that your daughter christened once as King Ralph. And you hold a fresh pad to your throat and climb softly to your sleeping bride to tell her before she sees the blood about the wounded bird, who chose anyway to keep on singing.

April/May 2022

Part IV.

TRAIN TIME

For Richard and Ianthe

"I will tell you about it because I am here and you are distant."
—Richard Brautigan

Toilet paper
caught white in trees
as egrets.

#

I'm fourteen again
doing a Brautigan.

#

Through 10,000 trees
sun sees his face
in the swamp.

#

Refinery across the plains
looks like an oil tanker
that sailed the farms
in a troubled dream.

#

We're all running down the line.

#

Iowa has hills
and they're outside the window:
long dirt road pale
through scraggle woods and suddenly
I live right there: I have a small fire
lit in the grate: I have a cane-back rocker:
haiku-reading dog: I use a Royal typewriter and listen
to LP records: Cat Mother
and the All-Night Newsboys: I never lock
my door: I never mourn
except for the train's passing.

Come find me.

#

A tall plume of smoke
Rises from the exact spot
Where the sun has set.

#

The train rides bareback
atop its own shadow.

#

5 drunk women sway
past to the lounge car for more beer:
each one 20 years older
than the woman before her:
a museum exposition
of time-lapse pictures.

#

Perfect degradation—
black bog simmers
in a prairie junkyard—
dead trees writhe
between shattered Chevies.
I want so much
to write that book.

#

When the magpie
Burst out of that tree
The branches
Kept retelling the story
For a minute.
#

Remembering my mother
Loving bare trees.

I wonder what trees
She sees now

In the world
She went to.

#

The last 3 tractors
we've passed, stood
motionless in those
dry and empty fields,
their drivers each

slumped and slack.
Did you hear a siren?
Everybody's dead.

#

Dead skunk out there
doing his best
the make his presence known
in that hot air—
what a poet.

#

The face reflected
in the window glass is of a grandfather.
The heart looking out
through the glass
is seven years old.

#

Trains sneak behind
careless towns who aren't paying attention
and look up their skirts.

#

Just remembered
in the Yukon
I reached into
Too Shy Lake
knowing I'd probably
not be back.
Just wanted
to shake hands.

#

For miles now
the only one driving
on that two-lane
is the sun.

#

Empty foundations gape,
ancient snaggletrees surrounding,
voice bulldozed into the grass.

#

Giant inflated rabbit!

#

A crow scolds
depressed pigs.

#

Horse
stops eating
looks up
at us
passing.

#

I tried to write haiku—
All I wrote were blurts.

#

Who put that picnic table in the blacktop lot?

#

We crawl. No bird
in the sky. Slant
light picks out
every blade of grass and
lends it glory.

Dad, are you watching
me?

#

Hai-choo: A Railway
Of Seeing.

#

wrecking yard

rust cars rest
atop other cars

toothy hoods
open to the sun

alligators

#

22 vending machines
in a vacant lot

I want to see the tractor
that harvests them.

#

Disillusioned Signs of America:
hung on a beanfield fence—
HAPPINESS
IS A
CROCK OF
BEANS.

#

Wrecked Corvette
Hides behind that barn
Embarrassed.

#

Dead ditches.

Flowing dirt.

Irrigate fields of dust.

#

One tractor
raises dust

lonesomest traffic jam
in 100 miles.

#

Mendota station, railroad museum.
We stop. We become a new display.

#

300 school buses
graze among scattered sheds
like orange
Aurochs.

#

Ah.
That cop
Has a tiny picnic
Beside the creek.

#

On a good day
I can't remember
Where I come from.

#

One small pine
stands like Christmas
beside a power pylon
shyly touching.

We ride the horn
through another town:
13 streets:
one minivan.

Mom inside it watches us escape.

All around her, forsythia
goes yellow
insane.

Like laughter.

#

mocking
bird
pray
for
me
I'm
on
my
way
home.

Notes and Acknowledgements

Thank you to the Master Blaster, Edward Vidaurre, editor/publisher/warrior extraordinaire. I am deeply honored to be included in the FlowerSong Press roster. The whole operation reminds me of the days when Xicano writers and poets and publishers pitched in to make books against all odds.

Thanks to the great homeboy, Juan-Felipe, who sent words of brotherhood and love while I was ill.

"Piedra" is the title of a song by Caifanes. It has many meanings for me. It first came to me in a dark time, and much of the last poetry book came from its shadows. And now I walked in a dark wood and got well from some illness, and the song and poetry feeling came back. "Quiero aprender amar."

"Train Time" was taken from notebooks on, well, train trips. On that trip I ate barbecue with Rush Limbaugh's cousins, and I also made the acquaintance of Kazakhstan's Chick Corea. It all started to feel like a Richard Brautigan story. Funny and sad. And that was one of the ways I got started, doing Brautigans, communing with Leonard Cohen records, writing in my notebooks on the floor of my bedroom or wandering the backyard at 3:00 with a family of skunks who threatened me, but never sprayed. Quite jolly, actually. Then Le Guin taught me how much of the Tao might be in such rambles.

Many of the poems in this book are new. "The Gospel of the Birds" is the newest and it is absolutely true.

Colleagues, friends, students and familia saw me through. Especially familia. Especially mi waifa. Our run is not over yet—a million miles ahead. Got a full tank of gas and my notebook tucked into my back pocket. I hope I make it to all of your houses before the snow.

—L.A.U.

Author Bio

Luis Alberto Urrea is a 2019 Guggenheim Fellow, a Pulitzer Prize finalist for nonfiction and the best-selling author of 19 books of fiction, nonfiction and poetry. He's been honored with a Pushcart Prize, an American Academy of Arts & Letters award and an Edgar Award. His most recent book is *The House of Broken Angels*, a NYTimes Notable Book of the year, finalist for the National Book Critics Circle Aware. His novel *Into the Beautiful North* is a selection of the NEA Big Reads program. Urrea's novel based on his mother's WWII experiences, *Good Night, Irene*, will be published in May 2023 by Little, Brown. He is a distinguished professor of creative writing at the University of Illinois-Chicago.

CPSIA information can be obtained
at www.ICGtesting.com
Printed in the USA
LVHW091928220223
740172LV00018B/1737

9 781953 447197